BEYONCÉ'S RENAISSANCE TOUR

in a
nutshell

A Record-Breaking Musical Journey that Redefined Live Performances

Felix Grayson

MINDSPARK
PUBLISHING

For the seekers of simplicity, the curious minds who crave the essentials without the fluff—this one's for you. Here's the story, in a nutshell.

"Brevity is the soul of wit."

— *William Shakespeare*

"Simplicity is the ultimate sophistication."

— *Leonardo da Vinci*

"Any fool can make something complicated. It takes a genius to make it simple."

— *Woody Guthrie*

IN A NUTSHELL'S PURPOSE

To provide quick, engaging overviews of pop culture, history, and trending topics, making it easy for readers to get the gist of any story.

IN A NUTSHELL'S MISSION

To deliver concise, entertaining content that educates and satisfies the curiosity of our readers and listeners in an ever-changing world of popular culture.

IN A NUTSHELL'S VISION

To be the go-to source for quick, digestible insights on the people, events, and trends shaping our world.

IN A NUTSHELL'S CORE VALUES

Simplicity: Making information clear, concise, and accessible.

Curiosity: Encouraging exploration and learning about diverse topics.

Entertainment: Providing facts in a fun and engaging way.

Timeliness: Keeping up with current events and trends.

CONTENTS

INTRODUCTION

The Renaissance tour wasn't just another concert series—it was a cultural phenomenon that captivated millions around the globe. As Beyoncé embarked on this record-breaking musical journey, she redefined the very essence of live performances. Her dedication to artistry, empowerment, and community transformed each show into an immersive experience, one that resonated with fans long after the final curtain call.

This book, *Beyoncé's Renaissance Tour in a Nutshell: A Record-Breaking Musical Journey that Redefined Live Performances,* offers a comprehensive look at the elements that made this tour so extraordinary. From the anticipation that surrounded its grand announcement to the meticulous preparation behind the scenes, every detail was carefully orchestrated to create a once-in-a-lifetime spectacle. The tour blended high fashion with groundbreaking stage design, merged music with visual storytelling, and celebrated the cultural roots of dance music, paying homage to the Black and LGBTQ+ communities that have shaped its legacy.

Beyoncé's Renaissance tour was more than just a showcase of musical hits; it was an exploration of themes that touched on empowerment, self-expression, and unity. Each chapter in this book delves into the various aspects of the tour—the intricate choreography, the dazzling costumes, the technological marvels, and the emotional fan reactions. We explore how Beyoncé curated her setlist to craft an emotional arc, how her fashion choices influenced global trends, and how the tour set new standards for live performances across the music industry.

This journey through Beyoncé's Renaissance tour also celebrates the powerful bond between the artist and her fans. The Beyhive's passion, dedication, and shared experiences brought the concerts to life, transforming each performance into a communal celebration of music, culture, and joy. Whether you were one of the lucky ones who experienced the tour live or you're reliving the magic through this book, you'll find that the Renaissance tour left an indelible mark on music history.

Join us as we explore the remarkable story of the Renaissance tour—a story of artistic vision, cultural impact, and the unbreakable connection between an icon and her fans.

CHAPTER 1: THE BUILD-UP TO THE RENAISSANCE

Beyoncé's Evolution

Beyoncé's journey from her early days in Destiny's Child to her solo career has been marked by constant evolution and reinvention. Starting as the lead vocalist of Destiny's Child, she captivated audiences with her vocal prowess, charisma, and relatable lyrics. However, it was her solo career that truly showcased her ability to transform and push musical boundaries. From the bold experimentation in her debut album "Dangerously in Love" to the assertive feminist anthems of "Lemonade," Beyoncé has continually explored new genres and themes.

In each phase of her career, she has embraced a blend of R&B, pop, soul, and hip-hop influences while also delving into political and social commentary. Her stylistic changes have been accompanied by increasingly elaborate visual elements, signaling her dedication to creating a complete experience for her audience. By the time "Renaissance" arrived, Beyoncé had firmly established herself as an artist who not only makes music but curates cultural events. Fans eagerly awaited her next move, expecting nothing less than a bold, immersive musical statement.

"Renaissance" promised a new chapter, one that would reflect her growth as an artist while honoring the musical legacies that had inspired her. As excitement built around the album, Beyoncé's evolution appeared not only as a testament to her versatility but also as a promise that this latest project would be a celebration of both her journey and the genres she would explore.

The Inspiration Behind 'Renaissance'

"Renaissance" was not merely another album release; it was a tribute to the history of dance, house, and disco music, genres that have shaped much of contemporary pop culture. Beyoncé drew inspiration from the sounds of the '70s, '80s, and '90s club scenes, embracing the vibrancy and freedom of those eras. The album echoed the carefree ethos of disco while infusing it with the modern sensibilities of house music. This fusion created a sonic experience that was both nostalgic and fresh, offering listeners a journey through time.

Beyoncé's deep appreciation for these genres

was evident in the album's rich soundscape. It paid homage to artists and movements that had championed self-expression, individuality, and liberation on the dance floor. From pulsating basslines to entrancing synths, the album captured the essence of dance music's ability to unite people and elevate the spirit. Songs like "Break My Soul" highlighted themes of resilience and empowerment, embodying the album's core message of finding joy and strength in self-liberation.

The inspiration behind "Renaissance" was also a nod to the underground club culture and the Black and LGBTQ+ communities that shaped it. Beyoncé honored these spaces as sanctuaries of creativity and freedom, amplifying their historical importance through her work. This layer of cultural homage gave the album a depth that resonated not only with her long-time fans but also with new listeners, igniting conversations about representation, inclusivity, and the power of music to create safe havens for all.

A Cultural Reset

Upon its release, "Renaissance" was immediately recognized as more than just an album; it was a cultural reset. Beyoncé had tapped into the collective consciousness, offering a project that felt perfectly timed for an audience craving liberation and escapism in a world filled with uncertainty. The album's infectious beats, coupled with its messages of empowerment, became a rallying cry for self-expression and joy.

"Renaissance" sparked discussions around music, identity, and cultural history. It pushed the boundaries of contemporary music by blending old-school influences with modern production techniques, challenging the status quo of what mainstream music could sound like. Critics and fans alike praised Beyoncé for her daring creativity, noting how the album reinvigorated a genre that had often been sidelined in favor of more commercial sounds.

The album also became a reference point for discussions on Black excellence and the reclamation of spaces that had historically marginalized Black artists and voices. Beyoncé's choice to celebrate dance and house music, genres rooted in Black and LGBTQ+ culture, was seen as a statement of pride and solidarity. In doing so, she created a work that transcended mere entertainment, serving as a call to action for inclusivity, self-empowerment, and the celebration of diverse musical histories.

Laying the Foundation

Beyoncé's strategic planning for the "Renaissance" tour began long before the album's release. True to her reputation for meticulousness, she left nothing to chance, carefully building anticipation through a series of subtle marketing moves and surprise elements. The promotional campaign for the album was marked by a level of secrecy and excitement that is characteristic of Beyoncé's brand. She teased elements of the album through cryptic posts, visual hints, and unannounced drops, all of which heightened curiosity and speculation among fans and media alike.

This calculated buildup extended into the planning of the tour. By the time the album officially dropped, the world was abuzz, and whispers of a tour began to circulate. Fans dissected every lyric, beat, and visual element of the album, searching for clues about what the live performances might entail. Beyoncé fueled this speculation, releasing occasional behind-the-scenes glimpses into her rehearsals and production meetings, hinting at a concert experience unlike any other.

The foundation for the tour was laid with an understanding of the album's themes and its cultural significance. Beyoncé was not simply preparing a set of songs to perform; she was crafting an immersive journey that would reflect the album's homage to dance, empowerment, and liberation. This careful, strategic approach ensured that when the tour was finally announced, it would be more than just a series of concerts—it would be a record-breaking musical journey that would redefine live performances.

CHAPTER 2: THE GRAND ANNOUNCEMENT

Unveiling the Tour

The announcement of Beyoncé's Renaissance tour was an event in itself, crafted with the precision and flair that fans have come to expect from the superstar. Unlike traditional tour reveals, Beyoncé and her team opted for an element of surprise, building suspense and excitement among her fanbase. The announcement came out of nowhere, sparking a social media frenzy. Fans and media outlets alike scrambled to share and analyze every detail of the reveal.

The unveiling was carried out through a series of cryptic social media posts and teasers. Starting with a single, enigmatic image on Beyoncé's official website, fans were left to speculate on what was to come. A few days later, a stunning promotional video was released, showing snippets of what appeared to be rehearsals interspersed with bold graphics bearing the word "Renaissance." This short yet impactful video set the internet ablaze. In true Beyoncé fashion, the announcement was layered with symbolism, hinting at the visual and thematic aspects of the tour.

Beyoncé's approach to the tour reveal was a masterclass in building intrigue. She maintained a level of mystery, giving just enough information to keep people talking but holding back the full scope of what the tour would encompass. As fans dissected the clues, excitement mounted, and the sense of anticipation reached a fever pitch. This strategic rollout not only caught the attention of her dedicated fanbase but also drew in casual listeners and media outlets eager to witness the next phase of Beyoncé's musical journey.

The Marketing Masterstroke

The tour announcement was followed by a marketing campaign that amplified the hype to unprecedented levels. Beyoncé and her team employed a multi-faceted marketing strategy that included social media engagement, exclusive merchandise drops, and subtle teasers. Every move was meticulously planned to generate buzz, utilizing the power of social media to engage with millions of fans across the globe.

Social media played a crucial role in the campaign. Beyoncé's accounts posted striking visuals and short clips that offered glimpses into the tour's aesthetic, leaving fans craving more. Hashtags like #RenaissanceTour and #BeyonceOnTour began trending almost immediately, fueled by fan discussions, speculative tweets, and meme culture. The strategic release of content was staggered, creating a steady stream of promotional material that kept the tour at the forefront of public consciousness.

In addition to social media, Beyoncé launched an exclusive line of tour merchandise. The collection included T-shirts, hoodies, posters, and even vinyl records, each adorned with the Renaissance motif. The merchandise quickly sold out, adding to the tour's allure. Beyoncé also collaborated with major streaming services to create official Renaissance playlists, featuring tracks from the album alongside her previous hits, reminding listeners of her expansive musical repertoire.

This marketing masterstroke not only reinforced

Beyoncé's image as a trendsetter but also engaged fans in a way that felt personal and interactive. The gradual reveal of details, coupled with the strategic use of scarcity and exclusivity, built a sense of urgency and excitement that few artists could match. By the time tickets went on sale, the demand was at an all-time high, and the stage was set for a record-breaking response.

Ticket Frenzy

The ticket sales for the Renaissance tour became a phenomenon, generating headlines and discussions across various media platforms. In line with the mysterious nature of the tour's promotion, Beyoncé's team released tickets in phases, with pre-sale events for dedicated fan clubs and credit card holders. This staggered approach was designed to manage the overwhelming demand, but it also added an element of competition that drove fans into a frenzy.

The ticketing process was not without its challenges. High demand led to crashes on ticketing websites, leaving fans frustrated and sparking conversations about the fairness of the sales process. Scalpers and bots swooped in to purchase tickets at breakneck speeds, only to resell them at exorbitant prices on secondary markets. Despite these issues, tickets sold out within minutes, and the official websites were flooded with traffic, reflecting the sheer scale of Beyoncé's global appeal.

Fan reactions were mixed. While some celebrated securing their coveted tickets, others expressed disappointment and frustration over the technical difficulties and inflated resale prices. Social media became a battleground of emotions, with fans sharing their experiences, both triumphant and heartbreaking. Despite the hurdles, the ticket frenzy underscored the tour's monumental status and cemented its place as one of the most anticipated live music events in recent history.

Beyoncé's team responded to the overwhelming demand by adding extra tour dates, giving more fans a chance to experience the Renaissance live. These additional dates, too, sold out almost immediately, further highlighting the tour's unparalleled popularity. In a world where live music was still finding its footing post-pandemic, Beyoncé's ticket sales proved that the desire for large-scale concerts was as strong as ever.

Post-Pandemic Concert Landscape

The Renaissance tour announcement came at a pivotal moment in the music industry. With the world gradually emerging from the pandemic, live performances were still navigating new norms and expectations. Concerts had become more than just entertainment; they were now seen as symbols of a return to communal experiences and joy. In this landscape, Beyoncé's tour announcement felt like a cultural reset, signaling a shift back to the energy and unity that only live music could provide.

Beyoncé's approach to her tour took these new realities into account. Health and safety were paramount, with venues implementing protocols to ensure the well-being of fans. The announcement emphasized not just the grandeur of the show but also the communal aspect of the concert experience, where music and human connection could flourish again. This messaging resonated deeply with audiences who had spent months craving such shared moments.

The tour also reshaped expectations for post-pandemic performances. While some artists opted for smaller, more intimate shows, Beyoncé went in the opposite direction, presenting a full-scale spectacle that harkened back to the glory days of live concerts. The grandeur of the tour became a statement in itself, suggesting that despite the challenges of the past years, the live music experience could still be elevated to new heights.

In doing so, Beyoncé set a precedent for other artists and the industry at large. The Renaissance tour became a blueprint for how to navigate the complexities of post-pandemic touring, blending spectacle with safety and engagement. It demonstrated that with careful planning and strategic marketing, live performances could not only return but also thrive in this new era.

CHAPTER 3: PREPARATION BEHIND THE SCENES

Choreography and Rehearsals

Behind every iconic Beyoncé performance is a rigorous process of choreography development and rehearsals. The Renaissance tour was no exception, requiring months of preparation to create the seamless, high-energy performances that fans have come to expect. Beyoncé's choreography has always been a signature aspect of her concerts, blending intricate dance routines with powerful stage presence. For the Renaissance tour, she aimed to elevate this even further, crafting routines that would not only entertain but also tell the story of the album.

Beyoncé's creative team, led by some of the industry's most renowned choreographers, played a crucial role in shaping the tour's dance sequences. The process began with brainstorming sessions, where they discussed the themes and emotions of the album. Each song was carefully analyzed to determine how movement could enhance its narrative. The team experimented with different styles, drawing on inspirations from house, ballroom, hip-hop, and even classical dance to create a diverse and dynamic choreography setlist.

Rehearsals were an intense and collaborative effort. Beyoncé, known for her relentless work ethic, personally attended and led many of the sessions, ensuring every step, gesture, and expression aligned with her vision. These rehearsals were not just about perfecting the dance moves; they were about building the stamina and synchronicity required for a live show of this scale. The dancers underwent physical conditioning, long practice hours, and technical training to execute the high-octane routines flawlessly. The result was a series of performances that flowed effortlessly, conveying the energy and emotion of the music while showcasing Beyoncé's dedication to her craft.

Designing the Experience

Creating an immersive concert experience was at the heart of the Renaissance tour's design. From the outset, Beyoncé and her team envisioned a production that would go beyond a standard concert, aiming to transport audiences into the world of "Renaissance." The tour's design process involved multiple stages, starting with concept development, where they mapped out the show's narrative, visual elements, and overall atmosphere.

Set design was a key focus, as it would serve as the backdrop for the musical journey. The stage was crafted to be modular, with movable platforms and various levels to allow for dynamic interactions between Beyoncé, her dancers, and the audience. Massive LED screens surrounded the stage, providing a canvas for visuals that complemented the music, from abstract patterns to symbolic imagery reflecting the album's themes. This setup allowed for a constantly evolving visual landscape, giving each song its unique atmosphere and aesthetic.

Lighting design also played a crucial role in shaping the experience. Beyoncé's team employed a combination of traditional stage lighting and cutting-edge technology, including laser effects, programmable LEDs, and spotlights that could track movements with precision. The lighting was meticulously choreographed to match the music's tempo and mood, enhancing the emotional impact of each performance. By integrating these elements, Beyoncé's team created an environment where music, dance, and visuals worked in harmony, enveloping the audience in the "Renaissance" world.

As the tour's design evolved, the team made adjustments to ensure it could be replicated consistently across different venues, from intimate theaters to massive stadiums. This flexibility was crucial for maintaining the quality of the experience regardless of location. Every detail, from the stage dimensions to the placement of speakers, was fine-tuned to ensure that audiences, whether in the front row or the back, felt the full impact of the show.

Costume Creation

No Beyoncé tour is complete without a dazzling array of costumes, and the Renaissance tour took this tradition to new heights. Fashion has always been a cornerstone of Beyoncé's performances, used not just for aesthetic appeal but as a means of storytelling. For the Renaissance tour, her wardrobe was designed to reflect the album's homage to dance culture, drawing from the bold, eclectic styles of club fashion, disco glam, and high couture.

The costume creation process was a collaboration between Beyoncé and some of the fashion industry's top designers. Designers such as Balmain, Versace, and Mugler were enlisted to bring the tour's visual narrative to life. Each costume was meticulously crafted, balancing glamour with functionality to ensure they could withstand the intense choreography and quick changes required during the show. The team explored various materials, including sequins, metallic fabrics, and sheer textiles, to create outfits that would catch the light and accentuate movement.

Beyoncé's outfits on the tour ranged from futuristic bodysuits to flowing gowns, each tailored to the tone of the songs and the overall concert theme. The bold designs featured dramatic silhouettes, vibrant colors, and intricate details, adding an extra layer of visual splendor to the performances. One standout look was a mirrored jumpsuit that sparkled under the stage lights, embodying the album's themes of self-reflection and empowerment.

Costume changes were seamlessly integrated into the show, with hidden backstage areas and quick-change techniques allowing Beyoncé to transform her look within seconds. This aspect of the performance added a theatrical element, as each outfit shift symbolized a new chapter in the concert's story. The costumes were more than just clothing; they were extensions of the music and movement, enhancing the concert's narrative and leaving a lasting impression on the audience.

Technical Marvels

Behind the scenes, the Renaissance tour was a feat of technical wizardry. Ensuring that each show ran smoothly required a dedicated team of sound engineers, lighting technicians, video operators, and stagehands, all working in unison to create a seamless production. The technical aspects of the tour were as meticulously planned as the choreography and set design, with countless hours spent on rehearsals and testing to guarantee that every element worked flawlessly.

Sound design was a top priority, as Beyoncé's powerful vocals and the album's complex production demanded a high-quality audio setup. The team used an array of state-of-the-art sound equipment, including wireless microphones, in-ear monitors, and a multi-channel mixing console to capture the depth and richness of the music. To ensure consistency across different venues, they employed a dynamic sound calibration system that adapted to the acoustics of each location, delivering a pristine listening experience for every audience member.

Visual effects were another cornerstone of the show's technical marvels. The LED screens used for stage backdrops were capable of displaying high-resolution graphics and live video feeds, allowing for dynamic, real-time visual storytelling. The tour also featured pyrotechnics, laser effects, and fog machines, all synchronized with the music and choreography to enhance the sensory experience. These elements were carefully choreographed with the lighting and stage movements, creating moments of surprise and awe throughout the concert.

Logistics played a crucial role in making the Renaissance tour a success. Transporting and setting up the complex stage design, sound equipment, and visual elements required precision and coordination. The production team devised an efficient system for packing, transporting, and assembling the stage in each city, ensuring that the tour could maintain its high standards of performance and spectacle no matter the location.

The technical execution of the Renaissance tour was a testament to the dedication and expertise of Beyoncé's team. By integrating cutting-edge technology with artistic vision, they created an immersive experience that captivated audiences and set a new standard for live performances.

CHAPTER 4: THE STAGE DESIGN AND VISUAL SPECTACLE

The Revolutionary Stage

The Renaissance tour's stage design was a marvel of innovation, setting a new benchmark for live concert experiences. Beyoncé and her creative team envisioned a stage that would not only serve as a backdrop for her performances but also actively engage the audience and amplify the album's themes. The result was a multi-level, interactive platform that redefined the dynamics of a live concert.

At the heart of this revolutionary design was a sprawling main stage that featured multiple tiers, walkways, and platforms. These different levels allowed Beyoncé and her dancers to move seamlessly between sections, creating a sense of depth and fluidity throughout the performance. The inclusion of elevated platforms enabled eye-catching choreography, with dancers seemingly appearing and disappearing at various points on the stage, adding an element of surprise and spectacle.

One of the standout elements of the stage was its circular design. Unlike traditional rectangular stages, the Renaissance tour featured a curved layout that gave the performance a 360-degree feel. This design allowed Beyoncé to interact with the audience from all angles, making the show more immersive and inclusive. Fans seated in every corner of the venue felt connected to the performance, transforming the concert into an intimate experience despite its large scale.

Interactive elements further enhanced the stage design. A central, rotating platform was used during key moments in the show, allowing Beyoncé to perform complex choreography while spinning effortlessly. This movement added dynamism to the visual presentation, giving the impression of a constantly evolving stage. Additionally, the stage was equipped with hidden trapdoors and hydraulic lifts that facilitated quick entrances and exits, enabling seamless transitions between different segments of the concert.

Visual Storytelling

The stage was more than just a physical platform; it was a canvas for visual storytelling that brought the "Renaissance" album to life. Massive LED screens enveloped the backdrop, providing a stunning display of visuals that ranged from abstract patterns to narrative-driven graphics. These screens were integral to the concert's storytelling, acting as extensions of the music and choreography.

Each song on the setlist was accompanied by its own unique visual theme, carefully curated to reflect the album's messages. During upbeat tracks, the screens erupted with vibrant colors and kaleidoscopic patterns, immersing the audience in a world of movement and energy. For more introspective moments, the visuals shifted to more subdued tones and symbolic imagery, enhancing the emotional depth of the performance. This dynamic use of visual elements created an evolving atmosphere, guiding the audience through the various moods and narratives of the concert.

Pyrotechnics and special effects added another layer to the visual spectacle. Carefully timed bursts of fireworks and flames punctuated key moments in the show, eliciting gasps and cheers from the crowd. The interplay between lighting, effects, and visuals was meticulously choreographed to align with the music's rhythm and beats, creating a multisensory experience that captivated audiences. Smoke machines and fog effects added an ethereal quality to certain songs, enveloping the stage in a mystical ambiance that complemented the "Renaissance" themes of transformation and self-discovery.

In essence, the visual storytelling of the Renaissance tour was a harmonious blend of art, technology, and performance. It elevated the concert from a mere collection of songs to an immersive journey, drawing fans into the world that Beyoncé had created.

Innovative Technology

The Renaissance tour embraced cutting-edge technology to deliver a concert experience that felt futuristic and groundbreaking. One of the most notable technological advancements was the use of augmented reality (AR). Through a dedicated mobile app, fans could access interactive AR features that synchronized with certain moments of the show. For instance, during specific songs, attendees could point their phones at the stage, triggering AR visuals that overlaid the live performance. This not only provided a personalized layer to the concert but also showcased how technology could enhance fan engagement in a live setting.

Drones also played a significant role in the visual presentation. During some of the tour's most spectacular moments, swarms of drones took to the air, forming intricate patterns and shapes above the stage. These drones were programmed to move in sync with the music, creating a mesmerizing aerial dance that left audiences in awe. At times, they arranged themselves into symbols and figures related to the album's themes, reinforcing the concert's narrative. This innovative use of drones added a celestial dimension to the show, blurring the line between art and technology.

Another technological marvel was the integration of real-time motion capture. Beyoncé and her dancers wore specialized sensors that tracked their movements on stage. This data was fed into the lighting and visual systems, allowing the on-screen graphics and stage lights to react dynamically to their movements. The result was a performance that felt alive and responsive, with visuals that seemed to breathe and dance along with the performers.

These technological elements were not simply added for spectacle; they were woven into the fabric of the show to enhance its thematic depth and interactivity. By incorporating augmented reality, drones, and motion capture, the Renaissance tour offered a glimpse into the future of live performances, where technology and artistry merge to create unforgettable experiences.

The Symbolism

Symbolism was a key aspect of the stage design, adding layers of meaning to the concert experience. Throughout the show, recurring motifs and symbols were subtly incorporated into the visuals and stage elements, reflecting the themes of the "Renaissance" album. One of the most prominent symbols was the mirror, used to convey ideas of self-reflection, identity, and transformation. Mirrors appeared in various forms—whether through reflective surfaces on the stage, visual effects on the LED screens, or even mirrored costumes worn by the performers.

Another significant motif was the circle, representing unity, wholeness, and the cyclical nature of life. The circular stage layout reinforced this symbolism, suggesting an ongoing journey of self-discovery and renewal. During moments of introspection in the performance, the central rotating platform was often bathed in soft, circular beams of light, creating the impression of a spotlight that both isolated and illuminated Beyoncé. This use of lighting and stage design emphasized the personal nature of the album's themes while inviting the audience to share in this introspective journey.

Butterflies were another recurring symbol, often appearing in the visual effects during transitional segments of the concert. Representing transformation and the emergence of one's true self, the butterflies complemented the album's narrative of liberation and empowerment. These visuals often accompanied songs that delved into themes of growth and self-realization, reinforcing the message that embracing one's authentic self is a powerful, beautiful transformation.

The inclusion of these symbols added depth to the performance, turning it into more than just a series of musical numbers. The concert became a narrative experience, with each symbol contributing to the overarching story of "Renaissance." Fans were encouraged to interpret these elements in their own ways, making the concert a deeply personal and resonant experience for each attendee.

CHAPTER 5: SETLIST AND MUSICAL JOURNEY

Crafting the Setlist

Crafting the setlist for the Renaissance tour was a meticulous process, aimed at creating an emotional and musical journey that would resonate deeply with the audience. Beyoncé and her team approached the setlist as a narrative arc, blending new tracks from the "Renaissance" album with iconic hits from her extensive discography. This thoughtful curation transformed the concert into more than just a collection of songs; it became an exploration of her musical evolution and artistic vision.

The process of selecting songs involved careful consideration of pacing, mood, and thematic connections. Beyoncé chose to open the concert with tracks from "Renaissance," immediately immersing the audience in the album's world of dance, liberation, and empowerment. These songs set the tone for the evening, establishing an atmosphere of high energy and celebration. As the show progressed, she gradually wove in fan-favorite hits like "Crazy in Love," "Formation," and "Love on Top," creating moments of nostalgia while highlighting her growth as an artist.

Beyoncé was intentional about the emotional
flow of the setlist. High-energy dance tracks
were often followed by slower, more introspective songs, allowing the audience to experience
a range of emotions. This ebb and flow mirrored
the album's themes of self-discovery and reflection, guiding the audience through a personal
and collective musical journey. By blending new
material with classic hits, Beyoncé demonstrated the continuity of her artistry, showing how
her music—past and present—contributes to
the narrative of empowerment and self-expression.

The setlist was also designed to showcase Beyoncé's versatility, moving seamlessly between
genres such as pop, R&B, hip-hop, soul, and
dance. This genre-blending was a reflection of
the "Renaissance" album's homage to musical
diversity, inviting the audience to experience
the full spectrum of her influences. In this way,
the setlist became a celebration of music itself,
emphasizing its power to inspire, uplift, and
bring people together.

Musical Transitions

One of the standout aspects of the Renaissance tour was the masterful way Beyoncé transitioned between songs and genres. Each transition was meticulously choreographed to ensure a smooth and cohesive musical experience. The team worked tirelessly to blend different tempos, rhythms, and styles, creating a seamless flow that kept the audience engaged from start to finish.

Beyoncé used a variety of techniques to achieve these transitions. In some cases, the shifts between songs were subtle, with the ending note of one track seamlessly blending into the opening beat of the next. Other transitions were more dramatic, involving tempo changes, instrumental solos, or spoken-word interludes that provided a moment of pause before launching into the next musical segment. These carefully crafted moments added an element of surprise to the concert, maintaining a sense of spontaneity while adhering to a precise structure.

The transitions also highlighted Beyoncé's ability to navigate different musical eras within her repertoire. For instance, she might shift from the house beats of "Break My Soul" into the sultry tones of "Naughty Girl," demonstrating her command of both modern and classic musical styles. These genre-crossing moments created an atmosphere of celebration, allowing the audience to experience the evolution of her sound and the timeless quality of her music.

By incorporating instrumental breakdowns, remixes, and vocal improvisations into these transitions, Beyoncé and her band infused each performance with a sense of freshness and originality. The transitions were not just bridges between songs; they were opportunities for creative expression, showcasing the artistry and dynamism of the live performance. This approach transformed the concert into a cohesive musical journey, rather than a simple sequence of individual tracks.

Live Vocals and Arrangements

Beyoncé's live vocal performances have long been a defining feature of her concerts, and the Renaissance tour was no exception. Known for her powerful voice and impeccable control, she delivered each song with a level of intensity and emotion that captivated audiences. What set this tour apart, however, was the reimagining of some of her classic hits through new vocal arrangements and interpretations.

Beyoncé approached her older tracks with a fresh perspective, modifying their arrangements to fit the tour's overall theme and mood. For example, a song like "Halo" might start with a stripped-down acoustic introduction, allowing her vocals to take center stage, before building into a soaring, full-band climax. These new arrangements breathed life into familiar songs, giving fans a chance to experience them in a different context. It also demonstrated Beyoncé's artistry and creativity, showing how she continues to evolve musically.

Her vocal performance during the Renaissance tour was marked by dynamic range and emotional nuance. Beyoncé effortlessly moved between powerhouse belting, sultry whispers, and intricate vocal runs, showcasing the full spectrum of her talent. The live renditions of "Renaissance" tracks were particularly noteworthy, as they captured the album's essence while adding the raw energy of a live performance. Songs like "Cuff It" and "Plastic Off the Sofa" featured extended vocal improvisations, allowing her to connect with the audience in an intimate and spontaneous way.

The presence of a live band added another layer to the vocal and musical arrangements. Beyoncé's band, composed of top-tier musicians, brought an organic quality to the performance, blending live instrumentation with electronic beats to create a rich sonic tapestry. This live arrangement not only enhanced the energy of the concert but also showcased the skill and artistry of her supporting musicians. The interplay between Beyoncé's vocals and the band's musicality created a dynamic and immersive soundscape, elevating the live versions of the songs beyond their studio recordings.

Audience Participation

A key element of the Renaissance tour's success was the interactive experience it provided for the audience. Beyoncé has always emphasized the importance of her fans, and this tour was designed to foster a sense of community and connection. Throughout the concert, she created moments that encouraged audience participation, turning each show into a shared celebration of music and empowerment.

Sing-alongs were a central feature of the concert, particularly during fan-favorite hits. Beyoncé would often hold out the microphone toward the crowd, inviting them to sing iconic lines from songs like "Irreplaceable" and "Formation." These moments of collective singing created an electric atmosphere, as thousands of voices joined together in unison. It was a testament to the deep bond between Beyoncé and her fans, highlighting how her music has become a soundtrack to many lives.

In addition to sing-alongs, Beyoncé included surprise shout-outs and acknowledgments of specific fans in the audience. During certain shows, she would pause between songs to interact with the crowd, responding to signs, outfits, and even dance moves she spotted from the stage. These interactions added an element of spontaneity to the performance, making each concert feel unique and personal. Fans felt seen and appreciated, enhancing their emotional connection to the experience.

Audience participation also extended to the visual aspects of the show. Concertgoers were encouraged to use their phone lights during specific songs, creating a stunning sea of twinkling lights that enveloped the venue. This simple yet powerful gesture transformed the audience into active participants in the visual storytelling, adding to the concert's communal vibe.

These moments of interaction not only energized the crowd but also underscored the themes of the "Renaissance" album—unity, joy, and self-expression. By inviting the audience to be part of the performance, Beyoncé turned the concert into a collaborative celebration, where music, movement, and emotion flowed freely between the stage and the crowd.

CHAPTER 6: FASHION AND ICONIC LOOKS

Beyoncé's Wardrobe

Beyoncé's wardrobe for the Renaissance tour was nothing short of breathtaking, serving as a powerful extension of the album's themes and the concert's overall narrative. Known for her bold fashion choices, Beyoncé collaborated with some of the most acclaimed designers in the industry to create a series of looks that were both stunning and meaningful. Each outfit was carefully crafted to reflect the different facets of the "Renaissance" era while also embodying the essence of Beyoncé's personal style.

For the tour, Beyoncé enlisted fashion houses such as Balmain, Mugler, Versace, and Valentino, among others, to design custom pieces that blended avant-garde aesthetics with classic glamour. The costumes ranged from futuristic bodysuits adorned with metallic elements to flowing gowns that evoked a sense of elegance and sophistication. These collaborations not only highlighted the creativity of the designers but also showcased Beyoncé's influence in the fashion world, as she worked closely with them to bring her vision to life.

Each outfit worn on stage was more than just a fashion statement; it was a deliberate choice that added depth to the performance. For instance, one of the standout looks of the tour was a dazzling silver bodysuit encrusted with crystals, designed by Mugler. This outfit, paired with knee-high boots and a cape, transformed Beyoncé into a modern-day goddess, exuding power and confidence. The reflective surfaces of the costume played with the stage lighting, creating a shimmering effect that resonated with the album's themes of self-reflection and radiance.

In addition to the custom designs, Beyoncé also incorporated elements of streetwear into her wardrobe, reflecting the album's connection to dance culture and club fashion. Oversized jackets, thigh-high boots, and bold accessories such as statement sunglasses and wide-brimmed hats added a touch of urban chic to her looks. These pieces served as a nod to the underground club scenes that inspired "Renaissance," bridging the gap between high fashion and everyday wear.

Costume Changes

One of the most captivating aspects of the Renaissance tour was the rapid and seamless costume changes that occurred throughout the show. Beyoncé has always been known for her quick transformations on stage, but for this tour, the costume changes were taken to a new level. Each change was meticulously choreographed and timed to align with the concert's narrative, adding an element of theatricality to the performance.

The costume changes were not merely transitions between different outfits; they were integral to the storytelling. As Beyoncé moved through the setlist, each costume change marked a new chapter in the musical journey, visually representing shifts in mood, theme, and energy. For example, a dramatic switch from a vibrant, high-energy ensemble to a sleek, all-black outfit often signaled a transition from upbeat dance tracks to more soulful, introspective songs. This interplay between fashion and music allowed the audience to experience the emotional arc of the concert on both an auditory and visual level.

The logistics behind these rapid costume changes were a marvel in themselves. Beyoncé's team of stylists and dressers worked behind the scenes to ensure each change was executed flawlessly. The stage design featured hidden areas that facilitated quick exits and re-entries, allowing Beyoncé to disappear momentarily before emerging in a completely new look. The costumes were specifically designed with quick changes in mind, incorporating features such as detachable pieces, Velcro closures, and hidden zippers to expedite the process.

These changes not only heightened the theatricality of the concert but also underscored Beyoncé's dedication to delivering a polished, dynamic performance. The costume transformations were a spectacle in their own right, drawing cheers from the audience and keeping the energy high. They added an element of surprise and excitement, as fans eagerly anticipated what Beyoncé would wear next, further immersing them in the concert experience.

Fashion Meets Performance

The fusion of fashion and performance was a defining characteristic of the Renaissance tour. Beyoncé's costumes were not simply outfits; they were extensions of the music and choreography, enhancing the storytelling aspect of the live show. Each piece was designed to complement the movements on stage, allowing for fluidity, drama, and expression.

During high-energy dance numbers, Beyoncé's wardrobe featured sleek, form-fitting bodysuits that accentuated her movements and allowed for ease of motion. These outfits often incorporated shimmering fabrics, sequins, and fringe that caught the stage lights and moved with her body, creating a dazzling visual effect. For songs like "Break My Soul," Beyoncé wore costumes that mirrored the song's exuberant energy, adding a layer of visual rhythm to the performance.

For more emotive and soulful songs, Beyoncé opted for costumes that conveyed elegance and sophistication. Flowing gowns with dramatic trains, sheer fabrics, and intricate embellishments created an atmosphere of grace and vulnerability. These outfits not only highlighted her vocal prowess but also added to the emotional impact of the performance. When singing ballads, the delicate movements of the gowns under the spotlight added a sense of intimacy and depth, drawing the audience into the moment.

The choreography was also designed with the costumes in mind, integrating elements such as capes, long sleeves, and headpieces into the dance routines. Beyoncé and her dancers used the garments as props, swirling skirts, tossing jackets, and manipulating accessories in sync with the music. This level of integration between fashion and movement transformed the concert into a full-fledged theatrical production, where every visual element was meticulously aligned with the narrative and emotional tone of the performance.

Impact on Global Fashion

Beyoncé's fashion choices for the Renaissance tour had a significant impact on global fashion trends. As one of the most influential style icons in the world, her on-stage wardrobe sparked conversations and inspired new trends in both streetwear and high fashion. Within days of the tour's debut, fashion blogs, magazines, and social media were abuzz with analyses of her outfits, dissecting every detail from fabric choices to accessories.

The influence of Beyoncé's tour wardrobe was particularly evident in the resurgence of certain styles and aesthetics. Metallics, sequins, and futuristic silhouettes quickly made their way into fashion collections and streetwear, as designers and brands sought to capture the glamour and boldness of the Renaissance tour. The integration of streetwear elements into her high-fashion looks also resonated with younger audiences, sparking a trend of combining luxury items with casual, everyday pieces.

Fans eagerly emulated Beyoncé's looks, creating a wave of "Renaissance-inspired" fashion across the globe. Social media platforms like TikTok and Instagram were flooded with fans recreating her outfits, incorporating elements such as oversized jackets, thigh-high boots, and mirrored accessories into their wardrobes. This phenomenon extended beyond individual fashion choices, influencing how people approached personal style and self-expression. Beyoncé's embrace of diverse fashion styles encouraged fans to experiment with bold and eclectic looks, celebrating individuality and creativity.

Beyoncé's collaboration with high-end designers also highlighted the intersection of music, fashion, and art. By wearing custom pieces from renowned fashion houses on stage, she blurred the lines between concert costumes and haute couture, elevating the status of performance fashion to that of high art. This approach not only reinforced her status as a fashion icon but also underscored the power of fashion as a tool for storytelling and cultural expression.

CHAPTER 7: FAN REACTIONS AND CULTURAL IMPACT

Fan Stories

The Renaissance tour left a profound impact on those who attended, with fans recounting their experiences as transformative and unforgettable. Beyoncé's concerts have always been more than just performances; they are events that evoke powerful emotions and create lasting memories. As the tour progressed, countless fan stories began circulating online, capturing the emotional and personal impact of the shows.

Many fans described the concert as a euphoric experience, where the energy of the music and the visual spectacle combined to create a sense of unity and joy. Some spoke of the anticipation and excitement that built up as the lights dimmed and Beyoncé took the stage, describing the moment as nothing short of magical. These personal accounts often highlighted how the tour provided an escape from everyday life, allowing fans to immerse themselves in an atmosphere of empowerment and celebration.

One of the most touching aspects of fan stories was the sense of representation and inclusivity they felt during the concert. Fans from diverse backgrounds shared how Beyoncé's performance made them feel seen and validated. Many attendees were moved by her acknowledgment of different cultures, identities, and communities throughout the show. Moments like the performance of "Break My Soul," with its themes of liberation and self-empowerment, resonated deeply, often leading to tears and overwhelming emotion among the crowd.

Viral moments also became a significant part of the tour's fan lore. Clips of Beyoncé interacting with the audience—whether by reading fan signs, joining in on dance routines, or spontaneously singing lines directed at specific fans—quickly spread online, becoming highlights for those both present and watching from afar. These interactions reinforced the personal connection between Beyoncé and her audience, adding to the collective memory and emotional impact of the Renaissance tour.

Social Media Buzz

Social media played a crucial role in amplifying the cultural significance of the Renaissance tour. From the moment of its announcement, the tour became a dominant topic across platforms like Twitter, Instagram, TikTok, and Facebook. Fans eagerly documented their concert experiences, sharing photos, videos, and live reactions that contributed to the tour's viral status.

The hashtag #RenaissanceTour trended globally, with millions of posts showcasing everything from ticket stubs and concert outfits to clips of Beyoncé's powerful performances. TikTok, in particular, became a hub for fan-created content, where users reenacted dance routines, shared their favorite concert moments, and even offered makeup tutorials inspired by Beyoncé's iconic looks from the tour. This wave of fan engagement created a sense of inclusivity, allowing those who couldn't attend the concerts to feel connected to the experience.

One of the most notable trends was the proliferation of fan-made videos capturing Beyoncé's audience interactions. These clips, often filmed from different angles throughout the venues, provided a multi-faceted view of the concert, showcasing the elaborate choreography, dazzling visuals, and Beyoncé's charismatic stage presence. The videos went viral, amassing millions of views and sparking conversations about the tour's grandeur and emotional depth.

Social media also became a space for fans to express their interpretations of the concert's themes and symbolism. Users dissected everything from Beyoncé's setlist choices to the meaning behind her costumes and stage visuals, creating a rich dialogue that extended beyond the concert itself. This ongoing buzz not only sustained interest in the tour but also highlighted its cultural impact, as fans actively engaged with the artistry and messages conveyed through the performances.

Cultural Conversations

The Renaissance tour sparked broader cultural conversations, transcending the realm of entertainment to address themes of empowerment, representation, and the future of live music. At its core, the tour celebrated self-expression and liberation, encouraging audiences to embrace their identities unapologetically. This message resonated powerfully in a cultural landscape increasingly focused on diversity, inclusion, and the affirmation of marginalized voices.

Beyoncé's homage to dance culture, particularly the contributions of the Black and LGBTQ+ communities, ignited discussions about the importance of recognizing and celebrating these cultural roots. Fans and critics alike praised her for using the platform of her tour to spotlight genres like house and disco, which have historically been shaped by these communities. This acknowledgment was seen as both an act of respect and a call to honor the legacy of dance music's pioneers, fostering a sense of solidarity and cultural pride.

The tour also sparked conversations about the future of live music in a post-pandemic world. Beyoncé's decision to go all-out with a massive, high-production tour, despite the challenges of the previous years, was viewed as a bold statement about the enduring power of live performances. It highlighted the concert experience as an essential aspect of cultural life, providing a space for collective joy, connection, and artistic expression.

Moreover, the Renaissance tour encouraged

discussions on the role of artists as cultural leaders. Beyoncé's use of her platform to address social and cultural themes—whether through her music, stage design, or audience interactions—set a precedent for how artists can blend entertainment with cultural commentary. This blend of artistry and activism inspired other musicians and creatives to explore how their work could contribute to meaningful dialogues and social change.

Beyoncé's Community

Beyoncé's fanbase, affectionately known as the Beyhive, has long been a community built on shared admiration for her music, artistry, and the values she represents. The Renaissance tour served as a unifying event that strengthened the bonds within this community, fostering a sense of solidarity and collective celebration. Concertgoers described the experience as being surrounded by like-minded individuals who shared a mutual love for music, empowerment, and self-expression.

The tour's inclusive atmosphere played a significant role in cultivating this sense of community. Beyoncé's performances were filled with moments that acknowledged and celebrated the diversity of her fanbase, creating an environment where everyone felt welcomed and valued. Fans embraced this inclusivity, expressing their support for one another both in-person at the concerts and online through fan forums and social media groups.

Pre-concert rituals became a defining aspect of the fan experience. Attendees shared stories of planning their concert outfits, often inspired by Beyoncé's iconic tour looks, and connecting with other fans in line at the venues. These interactions extended into the concert itself, where audience members danced, sang, and celebrated together. The shared experience of being part of the Renaissance tour created a collective memory that fans carried with them long after the final note was sung.

Online, the sense of community was equally strong. Social media became a space where fans could relive their concert experiences, share stories, and support one another. The hashtag #BeyhiveCommunity trended as fans posted photos and videos of their time at the concerts, along with messages of gratitude and joy. This virtual community provided a platform for fans worldwide to connect, reinforcing the idea that Beyoncé's music and performances transcended geographic and cultural boundaries.

Through the Renaissance tour, Beyoncé not only delivered an unforgettable live experience but also fostered a global community bound by shared values and the love of music. In doing so, she reinforced the power of music as a unifying force, capable of creating connections and sparking cultural movements.

CHAPTER 8: BREAKING RECORDS AND LEGACY

Record-Breaking Tour

The Renaissance tour was a phenomenon that shattered records and solidified its place in music history. From the moment tickets went on sale, the tour set new benchmarks, both in terms of demand and revenue. Tickets sold out within minutes for each announced date, prompting additional shows and the extension of the tour's run. This unprecedented demand was reflected in the staggering attendance numbers, with millions of fans flocking to venues around the world to witness Beyoncé's captivating performances.

Financially, the tour was a resounding success, grossing hundreds of millions of dollars in ticket sales alone. It quickly became one of the highest-grossing tours of all time, with several shows breaking records for individual venue sales. The Renaissance tour's revenue surpassed that of previous tours, highlighting Beyoncé's continued dominance in the music industry and the unwavering support of her global fanbase.

Media coverage of the tour was equally remarkable. Major news outlets and music publications closely followed every aspect of the concert series, from its announcement to its final performance. Headlines celebrated the tour's achievements, praising its artistic innovation and the unparalleled energy of the live shows. Social media platforms were flooded with statistics, fan reactions, and media analyses, creating a buzz that extended far beyond the concert venues.

The Renaissance tour also made history in terms of live streaming and digital content. Several concerts were partially broadcasted online, allowing fans who couldn't attend in person to experience the spectacle. These digital streams attracted millions of viewers, setting new records for online concert attendance. This fusion of live and digital experiences expanded the tour's reach and demonstrated the power of music to connect people across different formats and geographies.

Critical Acclaim

In addition to its commercial success, the Renaissance tour received widespread critical acclaim. Reviewers from major publications such as Rolling Stone, Billboard, and The New York Times lauded the tour as a groundbreaking artistic achievement. Critics praised Beyoncé for her ability to deliver a concert experience that was not only visually stunning but also deeply resonant and meaningful. The combination of elaborate stage design, intricate choreography, powerful vocals, and thought-provoking themes was hailed as a masterclass in live performance.

One aspect that garnered particular acclaim was Beyoncé's vocal prowess. Critics noted her impeccable control and dynamic range, emphasizing how her live renditions often surpassed their studio versions in emotional impact and technical skill. Her reimagining of classic hits, coupled with the new "Renaissance" material, showcased her versatility and growth as an artist. These performances were frequently described as "transcendent," "soul-stirring," and "electrifying," capturing the essence of what made the tour such a monumental event.

The tour's visual and thematic elements were also the subject of praise. Many reviewers highlighted the concert's ability to blend high fashion, cutting-edge technology, and cultural symbolism into a cohesive narrative. Beyoncé's celebration of dance music and its roots in Black and LGBTQ+ culture was acknowledged as both a bold artistic statement and a meaningful act of cultural recognition. The tour was seen as a powerful expression of artistry, inclusivity, and empowerment, reinforcing Beyoncé's status as a cultural icon and visionary.

Critics additionally commented on the tour's impact on the live music landscape. The Renaissance tour was viewed as a redefinition of what a concert could be—an immersive, multimedia experience that elevated music, fashion, and performance art. This critical reception cemented the tour's reputation as a defining moment in contemporary music, influencing how future live performances would be conceptualized and executed.

Impact on the Music Industry

The Renaissance tour's influence extended far beyond its immediate success, leaving a lasting mark on the music industry. One of the most significant impacts was its redefinition of live performance standards. The tour set a new benchmark for production value, showcasing how concerts could incorporate advanced technology, intricate staging, and multimedia elements to create an immersive experience. Artists and concert producers took note, leading to a wave of innovation in live show design and execution.

Beyoncé's use of technology, such as augmented reality and drone choreography, demonstrated the potential for integrating digital and physical elements in live performances. This approach inspired other artists to explore similar technologies, pushing the boundaries of how concerts could be experienced both in person and virtually. The success of these technological integrations also prompted discussions within the industry about the future of hybrid live-streamed concerts, providing a new model for reaching global audiences.

The Renaissance tour also influenced the fashion and merchandise strategies within the music business. Beyoncé's collaboration with high-end designers and the seamless blending of concert fashion with global trends highlighted the potential for artist-driven fashion lines and partnerships. This approach reshaped how artists viewed tour merchandise, transforming it from simple souvenirs into coveted fashion statements that fans eagerly sought out. As a result, artists began to invest more in the creative and commercial aspects of tour fashion, recognizing its cultural and economic impact.

Moreover, the tour's celebration of dance music and its cultural roots encouraged a resurgence of interest in the genre. Beyoncé's homage to the underground club scene and its ties to Black and LGBTQ+ communities not only acknowledged these cultural origins but also sparked a broader appreciation for the genre's history. This cultural recognition had a ripple effect, influencing music production trends and inspiring artists to incorporate elements of house, disco, and dance into their work.

The Legacy of 'Renaissance'

The legacy of the Renaissance tour is multifaceted, encompassing its artistic achievements, cultural significance, and impact on the future of live music. For Beyoncé, the tour represented a pivotal chapter in her career, showcasing her evolution as an artist and her commitment to using her platform to celebrate diversity, empowerment, and self-expression. It reaffirmed her status as a boundary-pushing performer and solidified her influence across music, fashion, and culture.

The tour redefined what audiences could expect from a live concert, setting a new standard for how music could be presented as a holistic, immersive experience. By combining intricate choreography, dynamic visuals, and a thoughtfully crafted setlist, Beyoncé transformed the traditional concert into a theatrical journey. This legacy has had a lasting impact on the music industry, inspiring artists to explore new ways of connecting with their audiences and telling stories through their performances.

Culturally, the Renaissance tour left an indelible mark by highlighting the importance of representation and community in music. Beyoncé's celebration of Black and LGBTQ+ culture resonated with fans and critics alike, fostering a dialogue about the roots of dance music and the value of inclusivity in the arts. This focus on cultural recognition and empowerment became a defining element of the tour's legacy, influencing how artists approached their work and the messages they sought to convey.

Ultimately, the Renaissance tour will be remembered as a landmark moment in live performance history. It not only showcased Beyoncé's unparalleled talent and creativity but also captured the spirit of an era—one marked by a longing for connection, joy, and artistic freedom. The tour's impact will continue to be felt for years to come, as it set a new precedent for what live music can achieve and how it can shape cultural conversations on a global scale.

CONCLUSION

Beyoncé's Renaissance tour was more than just a series of concerts; it was a cultural event that redefined live performances and left an indelible mark on music, fashion, and the collective consciousness of her fans. From the grand announcement to the final show, every aspect of the tour was meticulously crafted, reflecting Beyoncé's artistic vision and her commitment to pushing boundaries. It was a celebration of music, empowerment, and community, embodying the spirit of the "Renaissance" album and bringing it to life in an unforgettable way.

The tour's record-breaking success, critical acclaim, and cultural impact speak volumes about its significance. Beyoncé's innovative use of technology, the integration of high fashion with performance art, and her acknowledgment of dance music's cultural roots set a new standard for live shows. Her ability to blend spectacle with substance, to entertain while conveying powerful messages, solidified her status as an iconic and visionary artist. The Renaissance tour wasn't just a milestone in her career; it became a blueprint for the future of live performances.

Perhaps the most profound legacy of the Renaissance tour lies in the connections it forged. Whether through shared experiences at the concerts, the online fan community, or the broader cultural conversations it sparked, the tour brought people together. It reminded audiences of the unifying power of music, the importance of representation, and the joy that comes from celebrating one's authentic self. Beyoncé's Renaissance tour, in essence, was a journey that not only redefined live music but also empowered and inspired millions around the world.

As we look back on this record-breaking musical journey, it's clear that the Renaissance tour was more than just a moment—it was a movement. It reaffirmed the power of live music to transform, uplift, and connect us all. And while the tour may have concluded, its influence continues to resonate, setting the stage for future artists and performances to strive for the same level of artistry, inclusivity, and impact.

WANT MORE IN A NUTSHELL?

Curious for more quick, engaging reads that make complex stories simple?

The *In a Nutshell* series offers concise, entertaining overviews of pop culture, history, and trending topics—perfect for readers who love to learn, laugh, and stay informed.

Explore the full *In a Nutshell* collection and discover other books and audiobooks by **Felix Grayson**, published by **MindSpark Publishing**.

Visit **FelixGrayson.com** to see what's new,

what's trending, and what's next.

FelixGrayson.com 🔍

Big ideas don't need big books.

Sometimes, the best stories fit perfectly—in a nutshell.

ACKNOWLEDGEMENT

A heartfelt thank you to the incredible team behind Beyoncé's Renaissance tour, whose talent, dedication, and creativity brought this unforgettable journey to life. To Beyoncé and her entire creative and production crew, thank you for redefining the live concert experience and inspiring millions worldwide.

To the fans—the Beyhive—this book is for you. Your passion, stories, and unwavering support continue to elevate every moment of Beyoncé's artistry. You are the heartbeat of this journey, and it is your love and enthusiasm that makes the magic of these performances truly unforgettable.

Lastly, to everyone who has made this "In a

Nutshell" book possible—editors, designers, and readers—thank you for your contributions and for being part of this celebration of music, culture, and community.

ABOUT THE AUTHOR

 Felix Grayson has always been fascinated by the stories that shape our culture—from defining historical events to the moments in pop culture that captivate millions. With a lifelong passion for storytelling and discovery, Felix brings clarity and insight to complex topics, making them accessible, engaging, and fun to explore.

As the creator of the *In a Nutshell* series, Felix combines thoughtful research with concise sto-

rytelling to deliver quick yet meaningful overviews of the people, events, and trends shaping
our world. His mission is simple: to make learning enjoyable for everyone, no matter how busy
life gets.

When he's not diving into the latest cultural
phenomenon or uncovering forgotten chapters
of history, Felix enjoys connecting with readers,
sharing ideas, and exploring new stories—one
nutshell at a time.

www.ingramcontent.com/pod-product-compliance
Lightning Source LLC
Chambersburg PA
CBHW020420150626
46554CB00014B/2248